Maria Boxall

HARPSICHORD
METHOD

based on
sixteenth to eighteenth-century sources

Edition 11244

SCHOTT & CO. LTD. LONDON
48 Great Marlborough Street London W1V 2BN
B. Schott's Söhne, Mainz
Schott Music Corporation, New York

© 1977 Schott & Co. Ltd. London.
Printed in Great Britain by
Caligraving Limited,
Thetford, Norfolk.

ISBN 0 901 938 55 6

CONTENTS

INSIDE BACK COVER: **TEXT BOOK**

* *These pieces are printed out of numerical order to obviate awkward page turns*

'To Naomi'

1. First Piece

M. B. B.

2. Minuet

M. B. B.

3. Gavotte

M. B. B.

S & Co. 6970

4. Minuet

M. B. B.

5. Air

B. M.
Add. MS. 22099

John Blow 1649–1708

6. Minuet

Henry Purcell
1659-1695

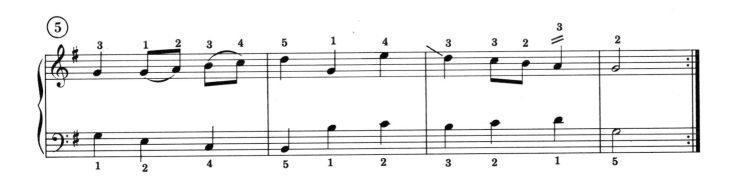

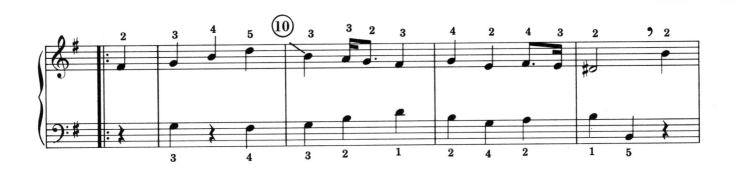

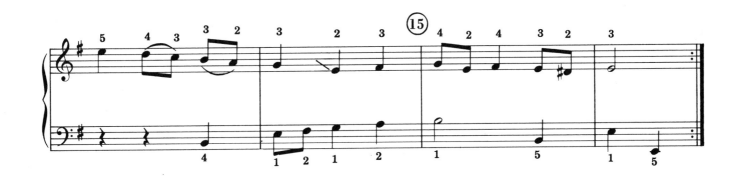

7. Minuet

B.M. Add. MS. 22099

John Barrett

MS. Bound with B.M.
copy of A Choice Collection of lessons
1696

8. Borry

H. Purcell

9. Menuet

George Frederick Handel
1685-1759

B.M.
R.M. 18. b. 8.

10. Passepied

G. F. Handel

B.M.
R.M. 19. a. 4.

11. Gavotte

B.M.
R.M. 19. a. 4.

G. F. Handel

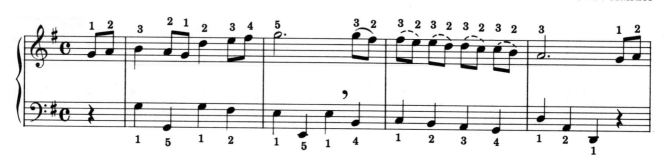

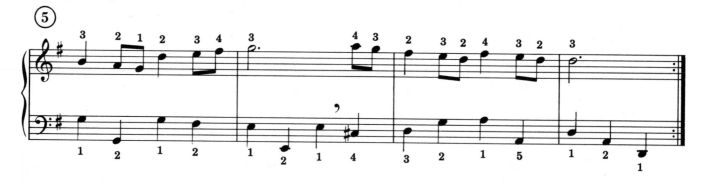

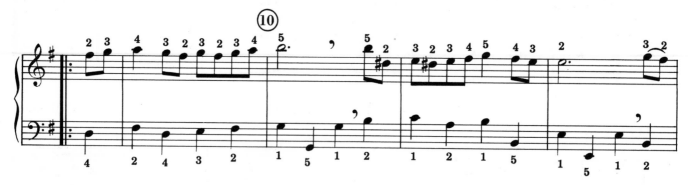

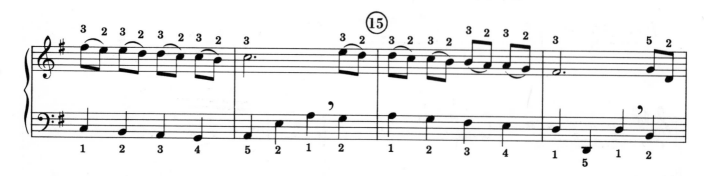

12. Air

B.M.
R.M. 18. b. 8.

G. F. Handel

13. Menuet

Anna Magdalena
Bach's Book 1725

Anon.

14. Menuet

Anna Magdalena
Bach's Book 1725

Anon.

15. Musette

Anna Magdalena
Bach's Book 1725

Anon.

16. Fuga

B.M.
R.M. 18. b. 8.

G. F. Handel

17. Les Tambourins

Quatrième Livre de
Pièces de Clavecin 1730

François Couperin (Le Grand)
1668-1733

Très légèrement

Fine

D. C. al Fine

18. Menuet en Rondeau

Pièces de Clavecin 1724

Jean-Philippe Rameau
1683-1764

19. Air

H. Purcell

Musick's Handmaid II
1689

20. Song Tune

H. Purcell

Pièces de Clavecin
1704

21. 2me Menuet

Louis Nicholas Clérambault
1676-1749

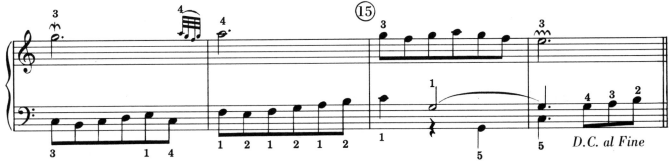

D.C. al Fine

22. Troisième Acte

Les Jongleurs, Sauteurs et Saltinbanques
avec les Ours et les Singes

Deuxième Livre de
Pièces de Clavecin 1716

F. Couperin

23. Menuet

Pièces de Clavecin 1707

Elisabeth Jacquet de la Guerre

24. Passepied

B.M.
R.M. 18. b. 8.

G. F. Handel

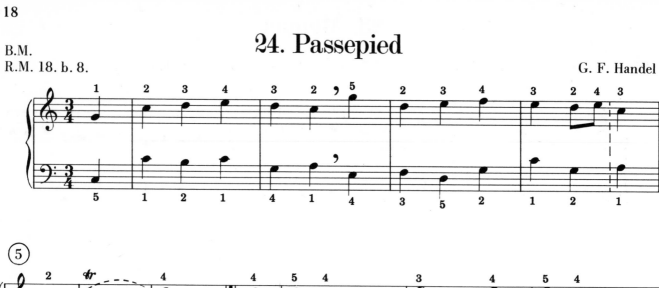

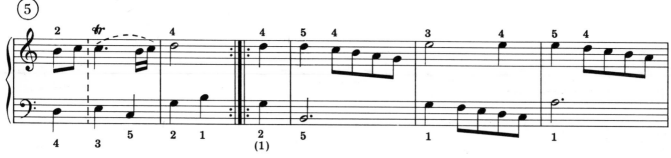

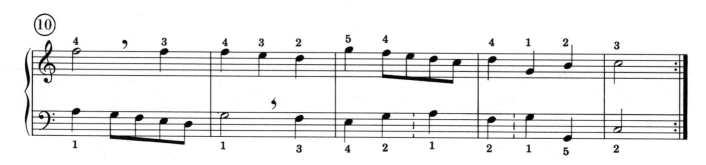

25. New Minuet

Musick's Handmaid II
1689

H. Purcell

Fine

D.C. al Fine

26. An Ayre

A Choice Collection of Ayres
1700

Jeremiah Clarke
ca.1670-1707

27. Minuet

Musick's Handmaid II
1689

H. Purcell

Fine

D. C. al Fine.

28. Minuet

A Choice Collection of Ayres
1700

H. Purcell

29. The Prince of Denmark's March

30. Rondeau

Quatrième Suite
from Pièces Courtes et Faciles

Jean François Dandrieu
1682–1738

Fine

D.C. al Fine

31. Gavotte

Quatrième Suite

J. F. Dandrieu

32. La Belle Javotte

autre fois l' Infante

Quatrième Livre de
Pièces de Clavecin 1730

F. Couperin

tendrement

Petite
Reprise

33. Les Coucous Bénévoles

Troisième Livre de
Pièces de Clavecin 1722
Coucou coucou

F. Couperin

A Choice Collection
1696

34. Prelude

H. Purcell

36. Churton's Farewell

Priscilla Bunbury's
Virginal Book

Randall Jewett

Musick's Handmaid II
1689

37. Prelude

H. Purcell

35. Les Lis naissans

Troisième Livre de
Pièces de Clavecin 1722

F. Couperin

Modérément et uniment

38. Prelude for the fingering

The Harpsichord Master, VIIIth Book
1722

Anon.

39. Praeambulum

W. Friedmann's Book 1720

Johann Sebastian Bach
1685 - 1750

40. Fabordone del primer tono

I : Llano

Antonio de Cabezón
1510–1566

41. Daunce

Early 17th Century

Anon.

42. The White Ribbon

Priscilla Bunbury's Virginal Book

Anon.

B.M. Add. MS. 30486

43. A Gigge

Anon.

44. La Volta

Fitzwilliam Virginal Book

William Byrd
1543–1623

45. Les Satires
(Seconde Partie)

Quatrième Livre de
Pièces de Clavecin 1730

F. Couperin

Vivement, et dans un goût burlesque

46. Applicatio

W. Friedmann's Book
1720

J. S. Bach

47. Preludium

Musick's Handmaid 1678

(after John Bull)

Susanne van Soldt MS.
1599

48. Preludium

John Bull
1562–1628

49. Corranto

Fitzwilliam Virginal Book

Anon.

50. The Maukin

Priscilla Bunbury's
Virginal Book

Anon.

Fitzwilliam Virginal Book

51. Praeludium

Anon.

52. Praeludium

Fitzwilliam Virginal Book

J. Bull

53. Brande champanje

Susanne van Soldt MS.
1599

Anon.

54. Prelude

B.M. Add. MS. 22099

J. Blow

56. Duo II

Obras de Música
1578

A. de Cabezón

55. Lo Ballo dell' Intorcia

Antonio Valente
ca. 1520 - 1581

57. Antiphon: Gloria tibi Trinitas

Oxford, Christ Church
Mus. MS. 371 f. 14

Thomas Tallis
d. 1585

58. A Fansye

The Mulliner Book

Newman

The note values in this piece have been halved

59. Prelude

H. Purcell

61. Verso del primer tono

Obras de Música
1578

A. de Cabezón

62. Verso del quarto tono

Obras de Música
1578

A. de Cabezón

Hymnes de L'eglise
1623

60. Ave Maris Stella
3e Verset
Canon in Diapente

Jehan Titelouze
1560–1633

The note value in this piece have been halved

The Mulliner Book

63. A Poyncte

T. Tallis

The note values in this piece have been halved

64. His Rest

Fitzwilliam Virginal Book

Giles Farnaby

65. Pavana, The Earl of Salisbury

Parthenia 1611

W. Byrde

66. A Pavyon

The Mulliner Book

Newman

The note values in this piece have been halved

67. Praeludium & Fughetta

J. S. Bach

Fughetta